My Magickal Flowers and Other Things

New and Collected Poems by

Heather Ann Shepard

For Marcus Shepard—

The love of my life and my greatest teacher

A monarch butterfly
On a green thread—
An angel spoke,

I listened.

Contents

Ode to A Winter Radish

You pucker your fuchsia mouth
Towards the sky
And are gathered from earth,
Held by farmers
And then mothers who create
Bouquets for tables
Roses in the sun
Petals scattered on the kitchen counter
A picture window
Framing a verdant summer day
You are the color of blood
On God's fingertips
After a long day in the fields

The Song of a Wood Wren

It has been said that
Beethoven heard his music
in the song of a wood wren....
so I try to hear my own music too.

My Winter Rose Garden

Who would think, a flower green?
Ruffled ladies, fair
Celadon and pink dresses everywhere
Asking the wind for a dance or two
And falling asleep when all is through
Under a quilt of whitest snow
Still, I ask each flower
In which direction did Spring go?
For yesterday was full of sun and daffodils
The grass was green and the wind was still
And the cherry blossoms dared to bloom
Yet, Winter decided upon its doom
So here I sit in my winter garden
With heavy heart
Waiting for Spring to start
Again.

If the dogwood bud's

Tightly shut eyes
Would open
They would see that spring
Is speaking full sentences
But they wait
To hear the frogs singing
First.

Lily of the Valley

I hold up the perfume to the sunlight
Streaming through my south window
In a month the oil and alcohol
Once cloudy, should hold clarity
I take off the glass top smelling the scent
And remember how flowers tell you
When they are ready to be picked
Revealing the tops of their heads
Under the new green
Even when there is snow
They want you to know
They are still there even though
Winter tries to hide them

Three springs have passed since I planted
The lily of the valley in my yard and
waited each year for her to reveal herself,
a shy white fairy
She is a part of my childhood—
The first perfume I received on my seventh birthday
Staying with me when I was afraid my mother
Would not come home
Something beautiful from something broken,
A strand of pearls needing to be restrung.

Oh Owl!

Oh, owl, whose eyes are
filled with the night's sadness, please
do not fly into
 my house and perch yourself in
the corner before I write!

Letter to Keats

Oh to love when one is young
The beating heart is held up to the sky
Waiting to kiss the lightning
Surging through the body
One rests in a field of bluebells
the elixir of rain coming down
Drenched in Earth's perfume,
absinthe air creating visions
I know your youth is pressed in glass
As the violets and butterflies we study
Our love compared to your words and images
Yes, I once had a first love, quivering
As the grass and wind make music only heard
By those who bend to hear
And in my mind it is still new
As the roses I placed in a book yesterday
To preserve forever.

Auburn Dream

Treetops
Take me to heaven
Let me breathe
This auburn dream
Burning sacred morning

The Philosopher King

Plato's words have been passed down
In our home
Over the dinner table
A necklace,
An ermine
Fashioned from ideas
Love of truth
Draped around our shoulders
It always start with a question
Whose petals scatter
Across the floor

And we scoop up the answers
With our cupped hands
And throw them in the air
Watching them fall to our feet.

Walk to the River

Walk to the river
to forget all of your pain
and lower your head,
let the tears fall from your eyes,
and mix with the river's voice.

An August Afternoon

My daughter morphs in the sunlight
When she dives into that other world
Where little girls become creatures of the deep.
When she emerges, she exclaims that she is a dolphin
Searching to find a home.
Then my son brings a lonely turquoise earring,
Along with a bottle cap and hair clip he has laid at my feet,
Small gifts drying in the sun.
And I am reminded that treasure is found
At the bottom of a community pool
As well as imaginary creatures whose names
I cannot pronounce
As I sit, a sparrow flies in, landing on the lounge chair beside me
Tilting its head as if it has something profound to say
to the August afternoon

But it can't be anything more important
than what my children have already told me.

Backyard Kingdoms

My daughter chases
toads down our driveway, catching
them and they climb up
Her forearms— initiation
into her backyard kingdom.

My son creates art
under a stand of pine trees—
twigs, leaves and needles
become tall buildings,
creatures chasing him into the wind.

January Girl

A cardinal
dresses up the fallen snow
hypercium berries turn their
faces toward the sun
My January girl
runs into the woods
to find deer tracks
or the path to a mystical land
she dreamt about the night before
I watch the rose clouds change shape
and think how the color is her namesake
so many shades her life will reveal
and then evaporate
into reality or dreams
that I will witness here or in heaven

Stillness at Green Lake

We stand as still as tree trunks
And I wait for my daughter
To point down to the water
That has gathered at the bottom of my sundress
We do not move so the water will stay clear
And we will see the blond fish swim around our ankles
And into the underwater knitting of lily pads
When they pass, we move forward
And dirt rises in silent explosions
To the top of Green Lake
A momentary reminder that we have been there
But will the fish remember?

Learning to Knit

Grandma Charlotte taught me to knit when I was eight…
We sat on a blanket at Sanibel Island
And my feet fidgeted in the white sand,
Heels marking my place.
Since she was right handed and I was left,
She retraced the steps, figuring out the opposite way
Placing her hands over mine
Showing me the rhythm
Until I moved the needles on my own.
Now, sitting on my front porch
During summer evenings
Sometimes creating scarves for my children
I knit without looking
Feeling the right tension
Closing my eyes
And the night air passes over me
Weaving my childhood
Into my son, my daughter

Little Buddhas

My son plays his toy accordion
And it drifts outside
With his singing laughter
And suddenly our kitchen is France.
It is quiet in our neighborhood
Except for the trees telling stories
And the children going
From house to house,
World to world
Trains whistle in the background—
Sudden enlightenment
These children are little Buddhas
Reminding me that this moment is life.

Black Walnut Trees

Aunt Judy took us into the rhubarb patch
outlining stands of black walnut trees on her farm.
And we picked the bitter stalks,
took our harvest into her ancient farm kitchen,
Mixed it with strawberries,
Making crisps or a pie
And as sparklers died out,
Stories about my grandmother Charlotte were revealed:
How she had many beaus in Joplin, Missouri
And met my grandfather in Lockwood.
Once the sky turned black,
My cousins and I took old mason jars
And tried to catch fireflies,
Attempting to hold light.

As a child, I believed God lived in those trees
And His divinity was revealed
In flickering flames behind glass.
As a woman I face those same trees
And pray to my Aunt Judy
What is it like to let go of gravity?

Saturday

At twelve,
Saturday was wash day
I ironed sheets, pillowcases and handkerchiefs using too much
starch
And then, with my earned ten dollars
Neatly creased in my pocket,
I would ride my mom's old three speed bike
To explore downtown Birmingham
Ending up in the local apothecary,
Eyeing the glass jars lined up
On dark wooden shelves
filled with lavender and Persian lilac soaps,
Dried roses and violets scooped into lace bags.
In that moment, I was an Edwardian lady
In fine Belgian lace wearing the kind of white gloves
we used in bell choir at church
And then, upon exit, I would walk slowly
Out of the store so as not to tear my dress
Or my imagination.

Fan Letter

    For Bono
When I was eleven
I sat at the chapel piano
And taught myself to play
Because we didn't have one at home.
Music drew me in
Words came to me
I knew I wanted to write songs
But I didn't know how
What I never realized is that
They already lived in the stars
They already lived in my heart
When I heard your music, your words
For the first time I knew
Where to find my own song
I would sit in the dark in my room
Your voice filling the space
A single candle
A book of words to be filled
And my own truth
My voice rising
Over the confusion of my youth
Over the hate and prejudice
I had the power to change
The world
one word at a time
What I know now is we all have the constellations within us
And we need to follow their light.

Running in Oberlin

As I run on this late spring morning
my feet are light
My ankles are not shackled
I run over the Underground Railroad
Where Prisoners of hatred, someone's so called property ran in
darkness
These holy streets have absorbed
Generations of protest
But do I remember on my daily pilgrimage
that I run with ease of breath?
No one is pressing on my back
To extinguish my words, my life
I am not running from something
With a 400-year-old tombstone on my back
I am running for the sake of my spirit
I am running to remember
That I do not understand
What I need to know
So I will listen and wait for the robins
to tell me where to go next.

Living Out The Last Scenes of My Life in a Garret

We are a cliche—
Artists in a Garret on Vineyard Street
Birthing creations with our hands, minds,
scraps of life torn from the garden of everything
We are an Eden
Flowers grow up the walls
cats at our feet and in our laps
Trying to coax the knowledge of the universe
From them but they will never tell us
You once told me that Jim Morrison died
Living in a garret in Paris
High above the mundane
Closer to the primitive and the poetry
Up here the church bells on the next block
Offer me redemption every morning
And I can find God in my harp,
In between each breath.

Witness Trees

I walk behind my daughter
Into the Hartwick Forest where virgin trees
Bear hundreds of rings and touch the sky
She tells me that the forgers of trails
Would mark trees along the way to show
Someone had been there, to set boundaries
Or to witness history
As I follow her, she looks up
I paint the light and lace
Of green in my heart
The shadow patterns shift
On her back telling stories
I don't have language to understand
These trees have seen so much—
The bravery of a woman's voice
Used to keep them alive.
So many witnesses across our land,
Silently seeing death traded for freedom
Young men hang on their limbs
Because color is more important
Than the idea that everyone has a voice
May she use her voice and may I use mine
To speak truth into the world and change
What is not right.

Upon Seeing an Old Beau

It could have been a
San Francisco beach
or an A&P parking lot
where you saw me—
twenty years reduced to minutia.

To look at us now,
one would never believe
that first kisses
produced snow stung cheeks
and modesty covered thighs,
now canals for new life.

Maps of years traced over our eyes,
stories of places seen,
dreams we breathed out
under Aurora's' flickering.

But your voice has the same
questioning tone
meandering through rings of sound
and pearls
fall to the floor,
astonished.

Papillion

I saw a butterfly
In early autumn
Resting on the dying leaves
Of a blackeyed susan—
Spindle legs
Pinching the
Leaf's tan curled edge
Waiting for the wind
To say
Go south.

Zen in a Winter Garden

You have told me this before:
Be still.
So, I sat in a winter garden

&
Counted the drops
Of melting snow
From the fountain
&
Saw the slanting hellebores
Pucker their purple mouths
Toward the winter blooms
&
Fallen green upon white—
Snowdrop petals chasing each other
As they release from my fingers
One for peace
Two for breath
Three for this very moment…

Nothingness Held in the Palm of My Hand

The universe begins its mediation in me
in one slow breath
then the flocks and dark matter disperse

I begin to understand
that the Great Universe has no name and
is everything and nothing
the origin is imbedded everywhere
Venus and Mars follow me on my drive home
There is male and female in the beginning
of no beginning.
Ah, Yes. This is so, my soul replies
To the open sky.

The Starling

The five am sky greets mourning doves
who have come back to the pine tree in my yard...

it has been five winters
that they have gone away
and six springs
they have returned

and their wandering wakes me
with a foggy refrain
I realize I had forgotten

and it causes me to muse
upon words that return to my memory
as a wave is pulled by the moon.

The tone of my mother's voice
when she read me stories
circles over my head
like a Hildebrandt's Starling

and I will always look for
the colors she described,
the colors I was certain I knew.

Crowns of Forsythia

When Spring came
Katie Evans and I
became princesses
of her backyard.

We wove crowns of forsythia
and were surrounded by fairies
that rested on the pale green leaves
forcing their way from branches
We discovered friendship
with small creatures that
crawled over our palms...
Even though our hands were small,
they held the world.

Quilt

When I was young, I gathered calico squares the color of summer trees and began to sew like my great grandmother did. When I wanted to imagine what she had been like, I would go into my parents room and run my fingers along the dimpling of her embroidery, feel the colors folded at the foot of their bed. I dreamt of laying my quilt over my daughter if she fell asleep on the porch or spreading it on the grass for a concert in the park. At night I opened my windows and laid on my bed, joining fabric with thread covering my knees and like a long letter, it was finished one day and had to be folded.

A Visit With Wallace Stevens

As I sit by the window, on this
summer day,
book of Wallace Stevens in my lap
I imagine you reading these
same poems... at a different
time in your life enveloped
by quiet midnight, when
youth's surly kiss was easier
to reach for.
In his poem about Key West,
the ocean speaks to me from
its four corners—
language of listless longing
Out of these tongues, I begin my search
for truth... a heart muscle's formation
knitted under and over bruises. I
know I have not worn innocence
in the same way as you
scales will shed in different patterns
from my skin to Earth's skirt swish
away, swallowed by the wind.
Life written with different
words
But in sleep, I keep my eyes open
to catch your wisdom as it sneaks
past my window in the middle of
the night hoping to
memorize the
fingerprint left the pane.

Summer Stories

In early morning,
I lie in my bed, hear rain,
in its scattered
voice, telling stories to trees
and I almost understand

Like wisdom in age,
the bamboo flowers late in
its life before death:
fragile straw hued lace against
the green of hundredth summer.

Ganymede

A stray iris—
smooth, milky
hiding behind Jupiter.
It is as if I can touch
this marble blown
out of the mouth of God

and play with the galaxies,
trying to figure
out the alignment
of reality.
Tonight, I rearrange my future
by connecting the dots
and coloring in
the empty spaces
with a palette
of reflected light
and fire.

Winter Story

It is late winter
the plum tree blossoms
outline the moon's face:
Spirit of the Plum Tree in
a woman's eyes gazing back.

Under the Acacia Tree

I sit under the umbrella of
the acacia tree
and let the voice of its field
speak to me....
and as the sky turns rose,
I become a part of its lace torn shadow
understanding its song.

So Unlike the Sun

So unlike the sun,
the moon, of dimpled star's dust,
sits, meditating
above the Earth's slumber and
knows that humans are observers too.

Today

I will sit
under the Japanese maple
It's shadows will cover my closed eyes
I will sit
And the butterfly will land
On my shoulder
And when I breathe
It will fly away
I will sit
And the breeze will sing a song
I have not heard in a long while
And it will lift away
I will sit
And my cat will lay beside me
Surveying its fiefdom
Focusing on a small creature
And depart
I will sit
And my thoughts , like radio
Frequency messages will pulse
Between clarity and static
Coming and going

Oh what friends there will be to meet!

Acknowledgements

"Quilt" appeared in *The Orange Room Review* and Silver Boomer Anthology *From the Porch Swing*

"The Starling" appeared in *Victorian Violet Press*

"Upon Seeing an Old Beau" appeared in *the Shine Journal*

"A Visit With Wallace Stevens" and "Ganymede" appeared in *Pirene's Fountain* "Letter to Keats" appeared in the *Taj Mahal Review*